Time Zones

Stories by
Stephen Dedman,
Chris McTrustry and Justin D'Ath

Ginn is a registered trademark of Harcourt Education Ltd

Linacre House, Jordan Hill, Oxford, OX2 8DP
a division of Harcourt Education Ltd

**Visit www.myprimary.co.uk to see a chart showing you all the
Pocket Reads programme information you will need.**

Miranda © Stephen Dedman 2000
It's About Time © Chris McTrustry 2000
The Natalies © Justin D'Ath 2002

From the Spinouts project developed by Paul Collins and Meredith Costain.

This book is copyright and reproduction of the whole or part without the
publisher's written permission is prohibited.

08 07 06 05
10 9 8 7 6 5 4 3 2
ISBN 0602 24319X / 978 0602 243197

Miranda illustrated by Grant Gittus
It's About Time illustrated by Peter Foster
The Natalies illustrated by Mitch Vane

Cover illustration by Marc McBride

Designed by Carolyn Gibson

Repro by Digital Imaging, Glasgow

Printed and bound in China through Phoenix Offset

CONTENTS

About Stephen Dedman

Stephen Dedman has been writing for fun since he was eight, and writes a short story every month. He has also worked as an actor, a teacher, an experimental subject and a used dinosaur salesman.

About the story

"For this story I took an idea from my list of things that scare me (falling) and a setting from my list of interesting places in the solar system. I wrote about a girl partly because I don't think there are enough science fiction stories about girls, and partly because I liked the idea of the character and the setting having the same name."

Stephen Dedman

Miranda

by Stephen Dedman

Of all the dumb things I've ever done, borrowing Mr Fujimura's spacesuit is probably the dumbest. Borrowing it without asking first certainly didn't help.

Leaning over too far at the top of a nineteen-kilometre-high cliff wasn't too smart, either. But what's the point of coming all the way out here and staying in the ship? Besides, Miranda and I were named after the same person, so I *had* to see the place, and the cliff was *much* more spectacular than anything we had on Earth.

Unfortunately, Mum and Dad didn't see it that way. They were really cross because I'd gone for a spacewalk without their permission while we were in orbit. So they'd grounded me by locking my suit away.

Mum had promised to take us to see the cliffs after she finished her work, but she tends not to notice the time when she's in the lab, and I was worried that she might forget, or leave it too late. Dad never argues with Mum, so there was no point in asking *him*.

Mr Fujimura's only a little taller than I am, so I borrowed his suit. He speaks English so well I'd never have guessed that his suit wouldn't too, and I didn't notice any problems until I was already outside the airlock. I tried talking to it in English, but it didn't seem to understand me.

Mr Fujimura's more than a hundred – so old that he can remember wars and plagues and scary stuff like that. But he treats us like we're his family.

He's invented all kinds of things. Dad told me that some of Mr Fujimura's own family died in a shuttle crash on the moon before I was born. And even though he's been working on ways of making spaceships and spacesuits safer ever since then, this was the first time he'd ever left Earth.

Our landing site was only a short walk from one of the cliffs, and the low gravity made the walk even shorter. Even in the suit, I weighed less than a kilo. If there had been any wind, I might have been blown away. (There wasn't, of course; Miranda hasn't any air.)

I was able to go right up to the edge of the cliff, and look straight down. If I spoke Japanese, I could've used the rangefinder to find out how high up I really was, but there was no way of telling. Because there wasn't any atmosphere, I could see clearly a long way down, but I couldn't see the bottom, even with the helmet light on. I might as well have tried looking up at the stars and guessing how far away *they* were. Still, the idea of being that high up was really exciting. I must have leaned too far, because the next thing I knew, I could see Uranus rising over the horizon ... except that it wasn't. I was looking *up* at the edge of the cliff.

The switch for the radio was where it should have been, so I didn't need to know Japanese to find it. The signal I got back from the ship was weak, and it took me a while to realise why. Miranda has no satellites and no ionosphere, so there's nothing for radio waves to bounce off, and I was several miles away from the ship, with a large cliff blocking the signal. I didn't know if yelling would help, but I couldn't think of any reason not to try it. "Help!" I shouted. "S O S. Mum! Dad! *Help!*"

I continued to fall while I waited for a reply. According to the clock in Mr Fujimura's helmet, I'd been plummeting down the cliff face for three or four minutes. But although the edge looked like it was further away, I still couldn't see the ground. In some ways, it was less scary than a roller-coaster. I *knew* I was falling, but I could hardly *feel* it. If I hadn't been sure that I was going to die, it might've been fun.

I wondered how big a crater I'd make when I hit the ground, and if they'd name it after me.

Probably not. Calling it Miranda would be silly.

I tried to work out how fast I was falling. On Earth, in one gravity, objects fall at just under 4.9 metres per second for the first second, accelerating at 4.9 metres per second until they reach terminal velocity. Even at that speed, I knew, falling just one kilometre would take nearly twenty seconds.

Miranda's gravity was a bit less than one percent of Earth's, but I knew I was falling faster than five centimetres a second. The computer in the helmet could have worked out the exact figures for me in a couple of nanoseconds, but even though Mum had taught me how to do maths in my head, I didn't think I'd have enough time.

The radio whispered, and I jacked the sound up. I thought I heard someone say, "Miranda?"

"Mum!"

"Where are you?" The voice was faint, but I could hear that she was angry.

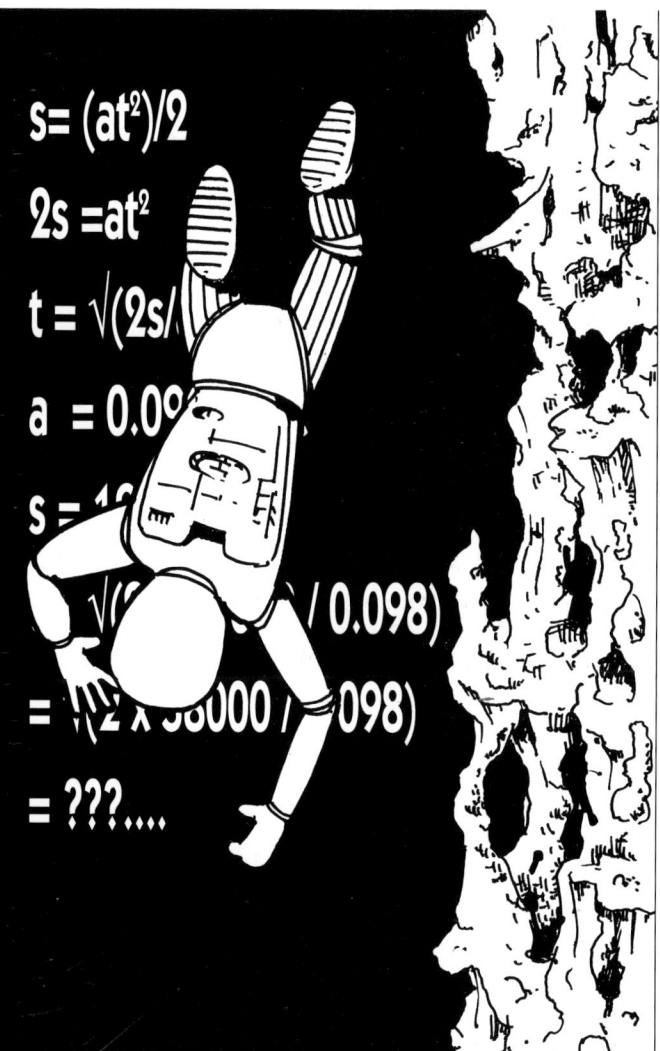

"Um ... You know that high cliff about half a kilometre from the ship?"

"Yes ..."

"I fell over it." No answer. "For real, Mum. No joke. Can you help me, please?"

Her reply was very quiet, but I heard something that sounded like "... suit ..."

"I took Mr Fujimura's suit," I said. "Can you tell him I'm sorry, and ask him if he can talk to it, please?"

I continued to fall, while Mum talked to me. I couldn't make out most of her words, but it was comforting just to hear another voice. A few minutes later, her voice became much louder and clearer, almost a shout. "Miranda! Can you hear me better now?"

"Yes!"

She sighed with relief, and turned the volume down. "Good. Your father and Dr Volkov are near the top of the cliff with a radio, and they've stuck an antenna out over the edge. They're trying to work out exactly where you are. Do you have your suit lights on?"

Oops. "Only the helmet light. I can't figure out some of the controls in this suit. They're in Japanese."

"OK. Here's Mr Fujimura."

"Miranda?" he said. He sounded sad.

"Mr Fujimura ... I'm sorry I took your suit without asking." It hadn't seemed like stealing at the time. "Can you help me, please?"

"I hope so," he said, "but I'm going to need you to be very brave. How long have you been falling?"

"About nine minutes."

"How far are you from the bottom?"

"I don't know. I can't get the rangefinder to work."

"Ah." He told me what to say, and I did, then he translated what the rangefinder said. I was still nearly ten kilometres from the ground. "OK. Do you have a full tank on your suit?"

"Yes," I said, a little hurt. Just because I'm twelve and was born on Earth doesn't mean I'm *stupid*.

"So you should have about nine hours of air left, if you use the rebreather ... good. Can you curl up as small as possible? Arms around your legs, head down?"

"Sure. Why?"

"I've built some special safety measures into that suit," he said. "If you say 'Chuta', it will become rigid. But don't say it until you've curled up like a ball. Do you understand?"

"OK ..." I locked my arms around my shins and brought my head down close to my thighs. "Chuta," I said. A second later, I felt the suit swell, and heard pieces lock into position. I could no longer move anything but my face, and I couldn't even move that very far. "Am I going to land safely now?" I asked, trying not to whimper.

"Ah ..." Mr Fujimura hesitated. "That depends how hard the ground is. If it's not too hard, you might just land, and we can dig you out later. But if it's as hard as we think it is ... well, you've gained a lot of energy by falling, and energy has to go somewhere ... you're going to bounce."

I gulped, and stared at the rangefinder, which was counting down rapidly. "Bounce?"

"Yes," he said. "Probably about half as high as you fell ... roughly nine kilometres. Then you'll fall again."

I closed my eyes. "And then?"

"The next bounce should only be four or five kilometres, then two, then one. You'll feel a bump each time, but it shouldn't be hard

enough to break any bones. We should be able to catch you by the time the bounces are down to twenty or thirty metres. It'll only be a few hours, and you have plenty of air and water …"

"A few hours?" I took a deep breath, then asked, "Can anyone else hear me?"

"Everyone can," said Mum.

"Can you shut them out? I want to speak to Mr Fujimura alone for a few seconds."

She hesitated for a while, then said, "OK."

I waited, then said, "Mr Fujimura, can I ask you two favours?"

"Yes."

"When this is over, can you teach me Japanese?"

"Of course," he said. "When I have time. What's the other favour?"

"Are you sure no one else can hear us?"

"Yes."

I looked at the clock in the helmet. "How do I go to the loo in this suit?"

About Chris McTrustry

In his writing career Chris McTrustry has enjoyed a second, third and fourth childhood writing children's fiction as well as television drama. He and his wife, son and daughter live in a large, chaotic but happy house.

About the story

"The possibilities thrown up by time travel have always fascinated me. A tiny change in the past can change the future in a big way. Now, that change could be bad or good ... We all know what the wise person will do. But time is a funny thing ..."

It's About Time

by Chris McTrustry

*You'll have the best holiday. Ever. Anywhere …
Any time …*

"Hey!" Dad shouted. "Our commercial is on the TV!"

"We're sitting right next to you, Alan," Mum said, sounding just as excited.

Call the Time Travel Agency for the time of your life!

"We're going to be rich!" Dad turned to me and smiled. "Terrific slogan, Susan."

Yes indeed, it *was* a catchy slogan – and true. We could transport people anywhere, in any time period. You see, Dad, Mum and I run the world's *first* time travel agency. Of course, time travel has been around for ages, but then Dad (Professor Alan Greaves to everyone else) stumbled onto "cloaking". Cloaking allowed people to visit any time in history, but not be *seen* or *heard* by the people in that time zone. So you have a cool holiday and don't get hassled by the locals. Cloaking also stopped people trying to rewrite history. Don't worry, plenty have tried and failed.

Speaking of history ... I had a project on famous explorers due the next day (believe me, it's a skill leaving things to the very last minute). I chose Captain Cook discovering Australia. Now all I needed was a little (time travel) favour from Dad ... Why own a time machine and not use it to help with homework?

I told Dad about my project. He told me off for not starting work on the project sooner and said this would be the one and only time he would let me use the machine for homework.

"I'll set the timer for fifteen minutes," Dad said, sternly.

"OK."

As he turned away to set the controls, I quickly flicked the switch on the cloaking device to "OFF". A no-no, I know, but I needed to talk to the Captain; get a few quotes. Stuff like that earned much-needed extra marks.

Dad hit the "GO" button and, in a twinkling, I was on the beach at Botany Bay watching a long-boat from the *Endeavour* striking out for shore.

Captain Cook was pleased to meet me and was very pleased to have discovered a new country for the King of England. But he didn't enjoy the heat or the flies and could I recommend somewhere he could get a cup of tea and a digestive biscuit?

I told him, sorry, I couldn't. I had my photograph taken with him (*that* took a little explaining); snapped some shots of the *Endeavour*, then, before I knew it, found myself zapped home.

"Happy now?" Dad said as I stepped out of the machine.

"Yes thanks. My project will be the best in the class." I edged over to the controls and flicked the cloaking device back to "ON".

"Good," Dad said. "A top mark will be a perfect birthday present for Mum."

Birthday? Present?

Aaaaaggghhhh!

Later that night, I lay in bed, plotting while I listened for signs Mum and Dad were asleep. At midnight, a deep, snorty snore blared down the hallway. Well, that was Mum asleep. Three minutes later, a wheezy whistle joined the blare. That was Dad. Both asleep.

Time for me to go to work. Or I should say, shopping.

I crept into the machine, set the date, time and location – and turned off the cloaking device. Twice in one day. This was becoming a bad habit. But I was desperate. Forgetting birthdays was a capital offence in our family. Besides, what harm could it do?

I landed in the local shopping centre and headed for the electrical goods store. As I raced into the store, I saw myself reaching for a portable CD player.

"You don't want that," I said, grabbing hold of the other me's wrist.

"Says who?" said the other me. Then she saw who had grabbed her and screamed.

"Keep it down."

The other me frowned at me. "What am I –
er, you – I mean me. What am I doing here?"

"Buying Mum a birthday present."

"But that's weeks away," the other
me scoffed.

"No!" I said. "You – we've had heaps of time
and not bought anything." I pointed at the CD
player. "I spent all my money on that."

The other me gaped at me. "I can see you!"

"Very clever," I said sarcastically.

"You're not cloaked!"

Gulp. "Yeah. So?" I held out my hand. "Give
me your pocket money."

"No way."

I put my hands on my hips. "We both know
what will happen if I don't get Mum a decent
present." And by decent I meant something
costing more than 50p.

The other me sucked on her top lip for a
moment, then nodded slowly.

"All right," she said, handing me her purse.
"But I'm keeping £1. For the lottery."

"Do you know the chances of winning?"

"Of course I do. I'm you." She paused. "Actually ... you're me."

I never realised how argumentative I could be.

"You should get a present too," I said.

"We both know I will," the other me said.

When I got home, Dad was waiting for me.

"What have you done?" he roared.

"N-nothing," I stammered. I held up Mum's present. "Just a little shopping."

"My computer has detected an approaching Time Fold."

That was a *big* no-no.

"You weren't cloaked, were you?"

I bowed my head. "No," I whispered.

"And you've done something in the past that's changed history."

"But I didn't do anything!" I protested.

Suddenly the room began to vibrate.

"Here it comes," Dad said.

There was a whoosh and a bright flash, then my clothes started *changing*. So did Dad's. His grotty flannelette pyjamas were replaced with silk pyjamas, flecked with strands of spun gold! Chunky, gem-filled rings appeared on each of his fingers and his hair had turned *bright green*.

A Time Fold is a change in history caused by a time traveller. In this case, me. *But*, if things turned out badly, the time traveller causing the Time Fold (me) had twenty-four hours to try and set things right.

"You know, Susan," Dad said in a posh voice, "I love being filthy rich!"

The Time Fold, *my* Time Fold, was *mega*-bad. The lottery ticket I bought had won. Not a bad thing, you might think, but Mum and Dad went completely crazy with our new-found wealth. They set up a chain of Time Travel Agencies. Unfortunately, some of the people they hired to run them were complete and utter crooks!

They used the Time Machines for their own benefit and travelled *uncloaked*.

"Woo," Dad said, grinning broadly, "that Fold was a doozy! My computer has calculated there have been twenty Time Folds a day since ..." He shrugged. "Whenever."

"Why don't you stop them?" I said.

Dad smiled and patted me on the head. "What for, sweetie? We've stayed rich. In fact, we get richer after each Fold. I think World War Five is really helping business."

All I could do was stare at him, mouth hanging open. *This* was my dad? No way. I wasn't getting stuck in this crazy world. I started all this nonsense with my uncloaked time trip, so I would have to fix the situation ... somehow.

If there were twenty Time Folds a day that meant I had just over an hour until someone else visited the past and changed history. What a lot of hassle for a birthday present! Birthday present ...? Of course!

I hurried to my bedroom, did some turbo typing on my PC, printed it out and raced back to the shop.

I planned a five minute trip. I switched the cloaking device to "OFF", hit the "GO" button and bingo, I was back in the electrical goods store. I saw myself enter the store (that's Me Number One) and head over to the CD players.

Moments later I (Me Number Two) raced into the store and grabbed Me Number One's wrist.

"Don't take her pocket money," I said, hurrying towards the other me.

Me Number One and Me Number Two turned sharply and screamed.

"What are you – er me, er –"

"Forget about who's who," I said. I turned to Me Number One. "Buy the player, OK?"

I turned to Me Number Two and pushed a plastic folder into her hands.

"Give this to Mum for her present – and some flowers. Don't ask questions. Just trust me."

Me Number One and Me Number Two nodded.

"Of course we'll trust you," said Me Number Two. "You're me – er, us – um ..."

Just then my time had expired and I was transported back.

As I edged out of the Time Machine, things looked normal (like before the Time Fold).

I heard footsteps approaching and Mum and Dad hurried in.

"Oh Susan," Mum said, smiling broadly.

I was relieved to see they were both wearing their usual (unrich) clothes. And Dad's hair wasn't green. Mum carried a plastic folder.

"The flowers are beautiful," Mum said.

Huh? Flowers? Oh! Of course!

"Happy birthday, Mum."

Mum kissed my cheek. "But this was the best present of all."

She opened the plastic folder and tapped the top right corner of the first page of my history project.

"An A plus?" I gasped.

"And well deserved," said Mum. "It was almost like you'd spoken with Captain Cook. You must have worked very hard."

I grinned and nodded. "You don't know *how* hard," I said.

About Justin D'Ath

Justin D'Ath's novels and short stories have been published in 19 countries. He has a dog called Pepper and always includes a dog in his children's novels.

About the story

"I once read about an African tribe where the people didn't like having their photos taken. They believed that the camera would steal part of themselves. That idea made a strong impression on me. I thought, what if there really was a camera that could take more than just photos?"

Justin

The Natalies

by Justin D'Ath

1) Too old to become twins

I didn't mind being an only child. There were no fights about who got to use the bathroom first, or which shows to watch on TV. I even had my own bedroom.

Then Natalie came along and everything changed.

Don't get the wrong idea – I like Natalie. But when you're twelve-and-a-half and an only child, you're too old to become twins.

Natalie thinks so, too. She and I have identical thoughts. Everything about us is identical. It's pretty confusing.

That's why Mum and Dad named her after me. (Or named me after her, Natalie reckons.) If we weren't both called Natalie, we would be fighting all the time about who was Natalie and who wasn't.

2) Concrograph

I should explain what's going on. Natalie is a concrograph of me. (She reckons *I'm* a concrograph of *her*.) A concrograph is like a photo, except it's real. You use a special camera invented by my mother. (Natalie reckons *her* mother invented it.)

Mum is a concrete artist: she makes statues and sculptures and models. She makes them out of just about anything she finds lying around. Mum is always looking for new ways of making models.

One day she worked out how to build a 3D camera. If it worked, all she would have to do was point it at something, click the button and she'd have a 3D model (or concrograph) of it.

It *did* work! And *I* was the first thing Mum took a concrograph of. That's where Natalie came from. (Or where *I* came from, Natalie reckons.)

3) Natalie 1 and Natalie 2

At school, nobody can tell us apart. Mr Hamilton tried calling us Natalie 1 and Natalie 2, but neither of us would answer to Natalie 2. It would be like admitting you weren't the real Natalie. *I* am, of course. (But Natalie reckons she is, too.) Now he calls us "Natalies".

"What's four times four, Natalies?" asks Mr Hamilton.

"Twelve," we both answer together.

4) Best and worst

The best part about having Natalie at school: I'm no longer bottom of the class in maths – Natalie is. (She reckons I am.)

The worst part: I lost my boyfriend.

5) How I lost my boyfriend

Robert Anshaw and I had been going out together for four months. We were the most famous couple at school. Everyone reckoned we'd be married one day. Then Natalie broke us up.

On her very first day at school (she said it was *my* very first day at school), I caught Natalie and Robert holding hands. I nearly died.

"Natalie!" I screeched. "Robert is *my* boyfriend!"

"Natalie!" she screeched right back at me. "Robert is *my* boyfriend!"

Robert looked at me, looked at Natalie, looked at me. "Wh-what's going on?" he stammered.

I grabbed hold of his free hand. "I'm the real Natalie, Robbo."

Natalie gripped his other hand. "*I'm* the real Natalie, Robbo."

"There are *two* of you?" Robert gasped.

"She's a concrograph!" Natalie and I both said together, pointing at each other with the hands that weren't holding Robert's.

"What's a concrograph?"

"Sort of like a clone," we explained.

"Aaargh! Clones!" Robert cried, leaping away from us as if we had bubonic plague. "I'm out of here!"

By the end of break, Robert was going steady with Pixie Ballantyne, and Natalie and I weren't speaking to each other.

6) The Natalies make up

"He was the grossest kisser," Natalie whispers during English.

"I know," I giggle.

Natalie leans closer. "*How* do you know?"

"I went out with him for four months."

"But," Natalie says, frowning, "*I* went out with him for four months."

Then it sinks in. Our four identical eyes bulge in horror.

"He *cheated* on us!"

Mr Hamilton's loud voice booms from the front of the classroom: "Natalies, are you two talking again?"

"It was Pixie," we both say together.

7) Beginner's luck

It's Sunday afternoon. Mrs Owen, our netball coach, is handing out the players' bibs. She gives GA to Natalie. I can't believe it.

"Mrs Owen, I always play Goal Attack!"

"*I* do!" says Natalie.

The coach glances back and forth between Natalie and me, a big frown wrinkling up her forehead. "Well, today you'll have to take turns."

So I sit fuming on the sideline for half the game. Natalie scores 22 goals. When my turn finally comes, I only manage eight.

"Beginner's luck," I say in the car going home.

Natalie turns round in the front seat and

gives me a nasty smile. "*You're* the beginner, Natalie 2."

"Dad," I yell, "Natalie's calling me names!"

Dad slows the car. "If you two don't stop fighting, you can both walk home."

"She started it," Natalie says.

"*She* did!"

8) Mental telepathy

We walk on opposite sides of the road. We don't look at each other. I'm thinking angry thoughts: *I wish she had never been concrographed*!

Suddenly I hear Natalie's voice inside my head: *I was* born, *Natalie. You're the one who was concrographed.*

Mental telepathy. I guess I should have expected it. After all, some twins are supposed to be able to communicate by thoughts, and we're closer than twins.

More alike, Natalie's thought-voice corrects me, *not closer*.

Get out of my head, Natalie! I think back at her.

You get out of mine!

For five minutes we keep our thoughts to ourselves. Then Natalie thinks loudly: *Isn't he gorgeous!*

I glance over to see what she's on about. It's a tall, black stallion in the middle of a paddock. I cross the road and join Natalie at the fence.

"I'd love a horse," she says dreamily.

"Me too," I agree.

Then we both have an idea.

9) Say cheese!

It's nearly dark when we return to the paddock. The stallion watches curiously as we slip through a gate and walk towards it. Natalie opens her backpack.

"Say cheese!"

Pointing Mum's 3D camera at the horse, she clicks the shutter twice.

10) Nobody lost them

Natalie and I are sitting proudly on our identical black stallions in the middle of the front lawn.

"Where did you get them?" asks Mum.

"We, um, found them," I stammer. It's the story Natalie and I have agreed on. Mum has told us we must *never* use her 3D camera.

Dad walks up and softly strokes my stallion's neck. "They're beautiful animals. Whoever lost them will be worried."

"Nobody lost them," Natalie and I both say together.

Mum and Dad glance at each other and shake their heads.

"You can look after them tonight," Mum says. "But tomorrow we'll have to find out where they came from."

11) Princes

After breakfast Mum rings the police station, but nobody has reported any horses missing.

"We told you," says Natalie.

"We told you," I say.

Mum and Dad look at each other and shrug.

Natalie and I go to school as usual. The day really drags. All we can think about is getting home to fuss over our horses. During maths we think up names for them.

"Mine's called Prince."

"*Mine* is!"

"Pixie!" Mr Hamilton roars from the front of the classroom.

"It was the Natalies," says Pixie, the rotten little creep.

12) They'll have to go

That night Mum and Dad are both in a bad mood. The Princes have trampled all over the vegetable garden and knocked down the washing line.

"A back garden is no place to keep horses!" says Mum.

"They'll have to go!" says Dad.

Natalie and I struggle to hold back our tears. All our lives we've dreamed of having horses, and now we aren't allowed to keep them.

"If we find somewhere else for the Princes to live …" Natalie begins.

"… then can we keep them?" I finish.

13) Brainwave

Natalie rides Prince and I ride Prince. When we reach the gate, Natalie jumps down and unlatches it. We are about to release the

Princes into the paddock with the original stallion when a four-wheel drive pulls up and out leaps a red-faced man.

"Get out of my paddock!"

"Can't we leave our horses here?" I ask.

"They'll keep your horse company," adds Natalie.

The man shakes his head. "I'm sorry, girls, but there's only enough room for one horse."

He's right. It's a very small paddock. But where else can we keep the Princes?

Suddenly – *ping!* – the Natalies have a brainwave.

14) Click, click!

At first light next morning, Natalie and I sneak back to the paddock. Nobody else is around. I catch the black stallion and make him stand behind a tree. Then Natalie points Mum's 3D camera at the empty paddock and clicks the shutter twice.

15) I told you *never!*

It's Mum's turn to drive us to school. Halfway there we become stuck in a huge traffic jam.

Natalie and I have exactly the same thought: *Uh-oh!*

Mum gets out of the car. Natalie and I follow her. When we arrive at the front of the queue, a huge crowd has formed. There are two paddocks in the middle of the road, completely blocking it. A third, identical paddock is over to the right where it has always been.

In all three paddocks stand three identical black stallions.

Mum stares for a long time at what's happened. Then, slowly, she turns around.

"Natalies," she says sternly, "I told you *never* to use my 3D camera!"

16) I'm going to miss ...

Mum doesn't say a word on the way home. She goes into the house and comes out with the 3D camera and a hammer.

"I'm sorry about this," Mum says to Natalie and me. She puts the camera on the driveway and raises the hammer. "It's the only way to undo what you two have done."

"I get it," says Natalie. "If you smash the camera, the two new paddocks will disappear."

Mum nods. "Along with everything else that has been concrographed."

"Not the Princes, too?" I say, alarmed.

"Yes, the Princes too, I'm afraid."

I wonder why there are tears in Mum's eyes. Then I realise what's about to happen. Natalie's going to disappear too!

Goodbye Natalie, I think. *I'm going to miss ...*

That's as far as I get. Out of the corner of my eye, I glimpse a flash of sun on the hammer as it